Practice Tests for the New Revised ABRSM Syllabus and Other Exams

Grade 5

DAVID TURNBULL

CONTENTS

Published by
Bosworth & Co. Limited
14-15 Berners Street,
London W1T 3LJ, UK.

Exclusive Distributors:
Music Sales Limited
Distribution Centre, Newmarket Road,
Bury St Edmunds, Suffolk IP33 3YB, UK.
Music Sales Pty Limited
20 Resolution Drive, Caringbah,
NSW 2229, Australia.

Order No. BOE100111
ISBN 978-1-84938-762-0

Printed in the EU.

Your Guarantee of Quality
As publishers, we strive to produce every book to the
highest commercial standards.
This book has been carefully designed to minimise awkward
page turns and to make playing from it a real pleasure.
Particular care has been given to specifying acid-free, neutral-sized
paper made from pulps which have not been elemental chlorine bleached.
This pulp is from farmed sustainable forests and was
produced with special regard for the environment.
Throughout, the printing and binding have been planned to ensure
a sturdy, attractive publication which should give years of enjoyment.
If your copy fails to meet our high standards,
please inform us and we will gladly replace it.

www.musicsales.com

BOSWORTH
part of The Music Sales Group

INTRODUCTION

As in all grades, success in aural is much more likely if listening skills are practised regularly rather than being left until the busy final weeks before the examination. To supplement work done in lessons, pupils can be encouraged to explore web sites and commercial CDs that offer suitable exercises, and to team-up with friends to test each other. They might also enjoy keeping a 'listening diary' of pieces that they've heard on the radio or on the Internet, noting points about features of the music that are relevant to the test in Section C (tonality, tempo, character, style and period, and so on).

Once it is time for more formal aural training, the late David Turnbull's popular *Aural Time!* series provides ample and highly regarded practice materials. This new edition coincides with the introduction of some small changes to the aural requirements of the Associated Board of the Royal Schools of Music examinations, effective from January 2011 onwards.

At Grade 5, the only significant changes are to questions in Test C(i). Here, there will no longer be any questions on form, and in questions on the character of the music examiners will ask something like, 'What in the music gives this piece its character?'. This is to make it clear that candidates must mention musical features in their response – things such as jolly dotted rhythms and staccato articulation, calm dynamics and a song-like melody, thick chords in a sombre minor key and so on.

A question about the style and period of the music heard in Test C(i) could be asked at Grade 5. This can be difficult for younger pupils, as identifying even broad stylistic periods (baroque, classical, romantic and modern) requires a degree of maturity and keen musical perception. A good starting point is investigation of the pieces that the pupil has learnt in the past, remembering that not all will be typical of their period. Encouraging pupils to dip into selections on radio stations such as Classic FM can also be beneficial – playlists appear on the station's website, allowing answers to be researched and checked. It is important to emphasise that *several* elements usually need to be considered for a correct identification of period. Some pupils will respond well to the idea of being a 'musical detective', looking for clues and deciding which are important to solving the case and which could turn out to be 'red herrings'.

Pupils who have worked through the earlier grades should be gaining confidence by now in tests that require a sung response. However, for those who find this a worry, it is worth emphasising that the examiner is only interested in accurate pitch – vocal tone does not matter. Boys with changing voices may sing an octave lower and candidates may whistle or hum if that is easier. Remember that answers to Test A can be played rather than sung, in which case the examiner will name the key chord and starting note.

In Test B, pupils should be encouraged not to rush through the six notes required – each should be sustained for a second or two (something that nervous singers often find difficult). Teachers should interrupt the singing if any note is incorrectly pitched by saying, for example, 'no, the third note should be …' and then playing the correct pitch. Pupils need to be aware that a similar interruption is likely to occur in the examination, as this type of test can rarely be completed accurately once an interval has been wrongly pitched. Those that find this type of test difficult will benefit by starting with the 36 very simple, graded examples in Section B of *Aural Time!* Grade 4.

Paul Terry
London, 2010

Test A. Memorising Melodies

GRADE 5

These melodies will be played twice. The keychord and the starting note will be played and named, and the pulse tapped. Then pupils must **either** sing **or** play back the melodies.

Sometimes, pupils find at first that they cannot remember all of a melody. Teachers may like to divide some melodies into smaller phrases to help in the beginning stages. Possible phrasing has been indicated in such cases.

2

Test B. Sight-Singing in Free Time

These exercises are to be sung at sight in free time. The keychord and the keynote will be given. Any wrong notes will be corrected at the keyboard.

In examinations they are sung to vowels or 'lah' but they also make excellent practice for general aural development for GCSE and other work if they are sung to their letter names or sol-fa names.

Tests are written in treble and bass clefs, and pupils may choose which clef they wish to use in an examination. However, when practising pupils can also be encouraged to sing from *both* clefs, transposing the starting note down or up an octave as necessary, so that note reading becomes equally fluent in treble and the bass clefs. As well as practising these tests with their teacher, pupils can also be encouraged to practise them on their own, giving themselves keychords and checking their notes with their instrument.

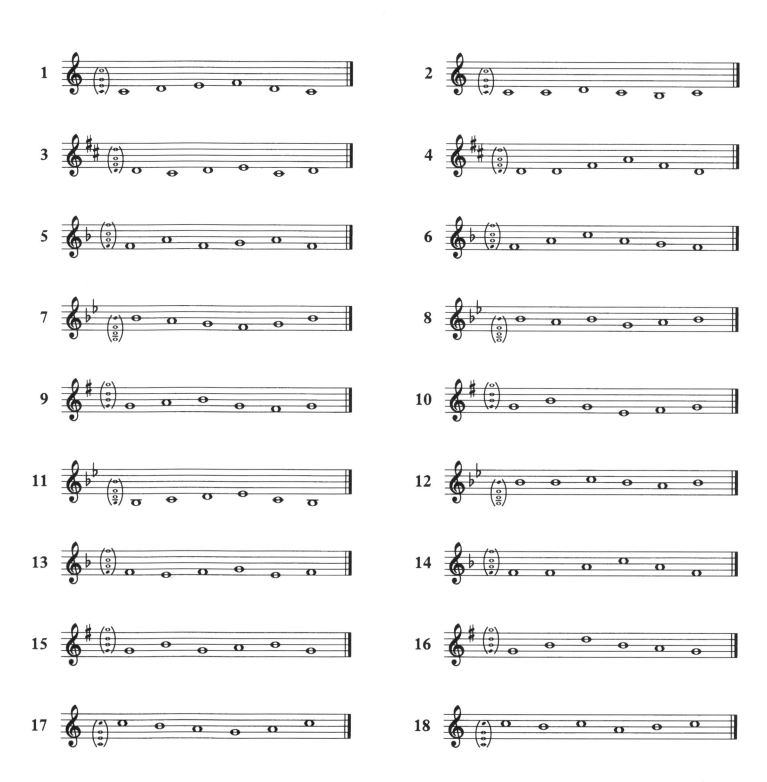

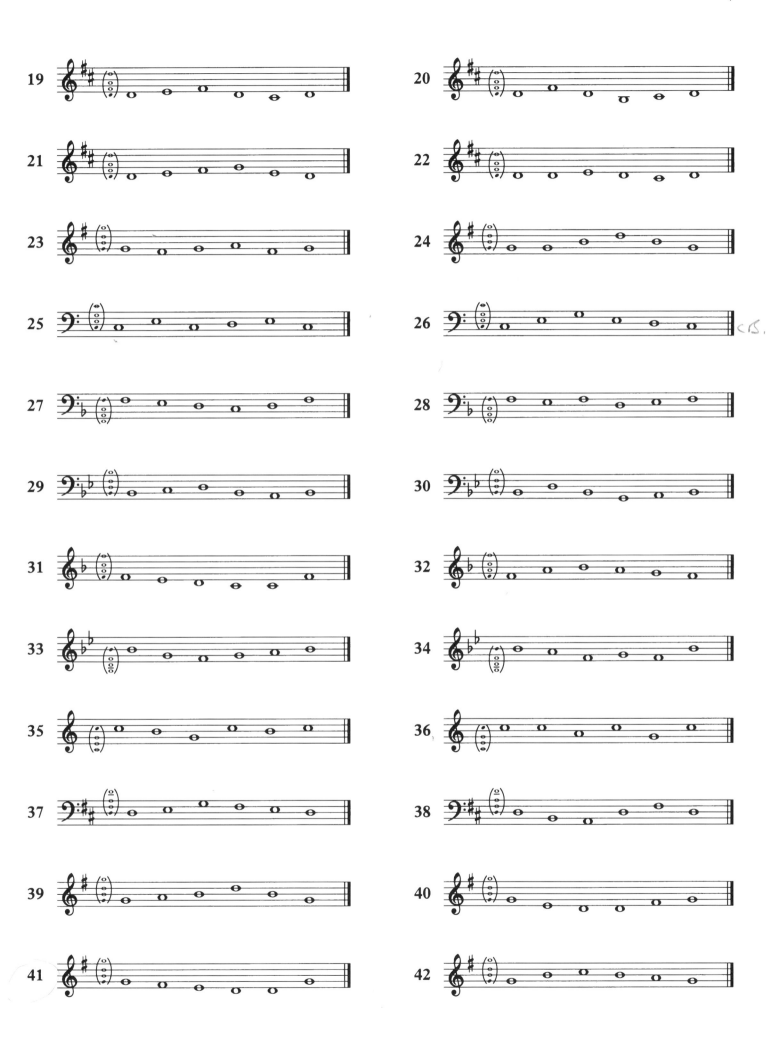

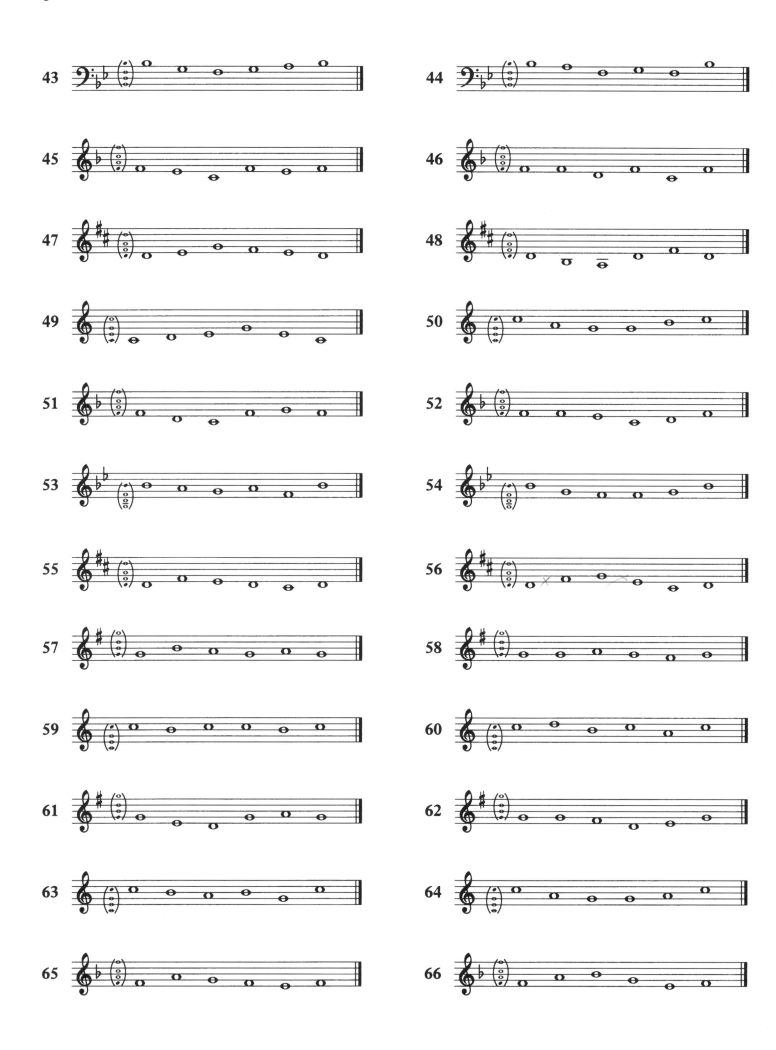

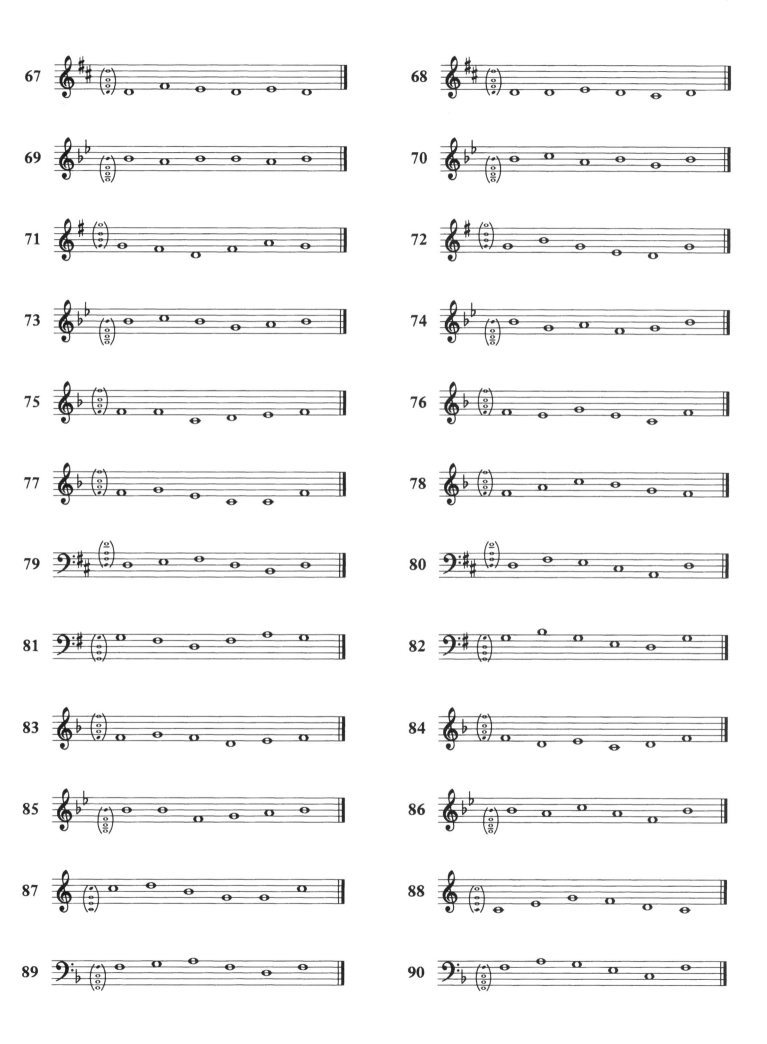

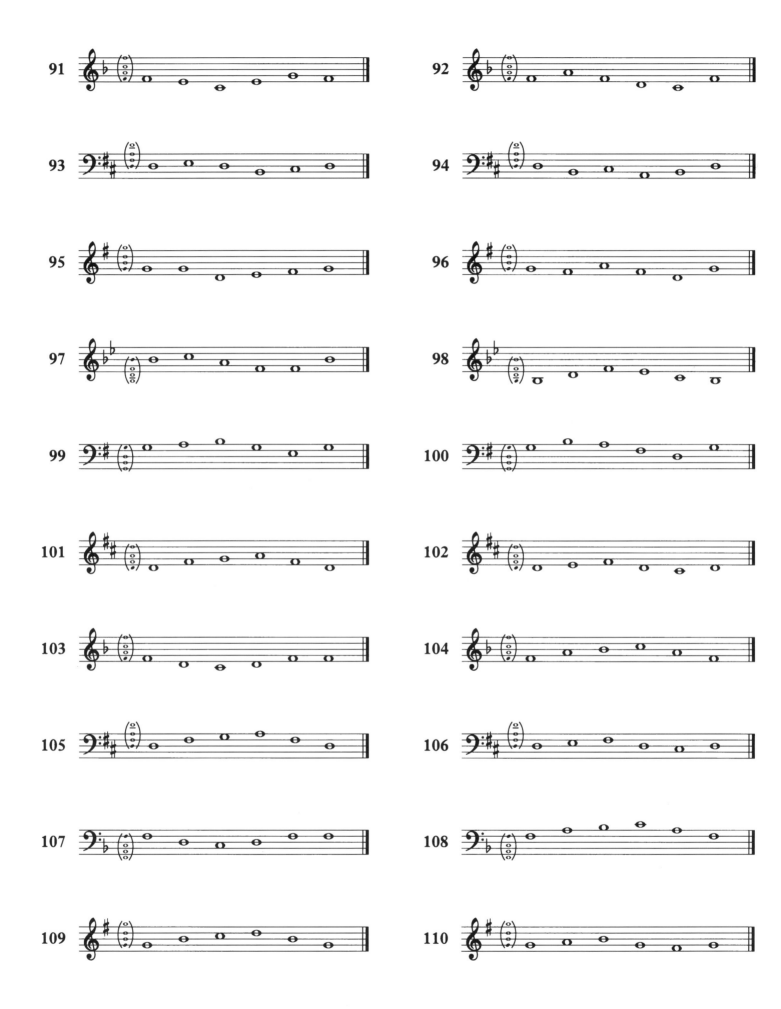

Test C1. Recognising Features.

To the pupil.

You will be asked to comment on two of the following features of pieces in this section:

dynamics (*p/f*), and **gradation of dynamics** (*crescendo/diminuendo*),
articulation of notes (*legato/staccato*);
tempo including changes to tempo (*rallentando, accelerando* etc.);
Whether the **tonality** (key) is major or minor;
the **character** of the music played.
the **style** and **period** of the music

You will be told which two features you will be questioned on before the piece is played.

Test C2. Clapping rhythms

Your teacher will play twice a short extract from the piece used in C1. You must clap back its rhythm, and say if it is in two, three of four time.

To the teacher. For the C2 clapping, two phrases are printed from which you can choose **one**. Comments on the style and period of each example are on p.30.

C1 *Questions*
    a. How many times does the opening four-bar phrase in the **melody** appear?
    b. Where is there a change in **tonality** from major to minor?
    c. Does the **tempo** change? If so, where?
    d. Are the **dynamics** mainly loud, or soft? If there is a change, where did it occur?

C2 Clap this extract, which will be played twice. After you have clapped it, say if it is in two time, three time or four time.

C1 *Questions*

    a. Is the **texture** of this piece mostly harmonic, or contrapuntal?

    b. Does the piece start in major or minor **tonality**? Is there any change later?

    c. Is the **articulation** of the notes mostly *staccato* or *legato*?

    d. Describe the **character** of the music.

    e. In what **period** do you think it was written?

C2 Clap this extract, which will be played twice. After you have clapped it, say if it is in two time, three time or four time.

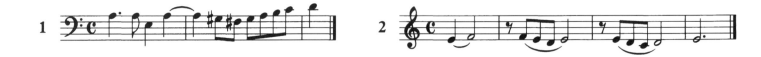

Chopin (1810-1849)

C1 *Questions*
a. Is the **texture** of this piece mostly harmonic, or contrapuntal?
b. **Form.** How many sections are there? Were any repeated?
c. Describe the **dynamics** of the piece.
d. What is the **character** of this piece? Is the **tonality** mostly major, or minor?
e. In what **period** might it have been written?

C2 Clap this extract, which will be played twice. After you have clapped it, say if it is in two time, three time or four time.

J.S. Bach (1685-1750)

C1 *Questions*

a. Describe the **form** of the example.
b. Is the **tonality** major or minor?
c. Is the **tempo** steady, or does it change?
d. Is the **articulation** *legato* or *staccato*?
e. What is the **character** of this piece?

C2 Clap this extract, which will be played twice. After you have clapped it, say if it is in two time, three time or four time.

Allegretto

Schubert (1797-1828)

C1 *Questions*
a. Is this mostly homophonic or contrapuntal in **texture**?
b. Is the **tonality** major or minor at the beginning? And at the end?
c. Is the **articulation** of notes *legato*, *staccato*, or a mixture of both?
d. Describe the **dynamics** of the piece.
e. What do you think is the **style** and **period** of the piece?

C2 Clap this extract, which will be played twice. After you have clapped it, say if it is in two time, three time or four time.

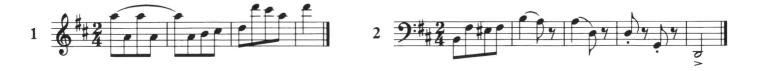

C1 Questions
  a. Is the **tempo** strict, or free? What happens at the end?
  b. Comment of the **dynamics** of this music.
  c. Is the **harmony** unusual?
  d. Comment on the **character** of the music.
  e. In which **period** might it have been written?

C2 Clap this extract, which will be played twice. After you have clapped it, say if it is in two time, three time or four time.

C1 *Questions*

    a. Is the **articulation** mostly *legato* or *staccato*?

    b. Describe the **dynamics**.

    c. Does the opening **melody** always occur in the treble? If not, explain.

    d. Is the **tonality** major, or minor?

    e. What do you think is the **character** of this piecce?

C2 Clap this extract, which will be played twice. After you have clapped it, say if it is in two time, three time or four time.

Schumann (1810-1856)

C1 *Questions*

 a. Is the **texture** of this piece mostly homophonic, or contrapuntal?
 b. Does the **tempo** change? Is so, where?
 c. Describe the **dynamics**.
 d. Describe the **character** of the music?
 e. In what **period** might this have been written?

C2 Clap this extract, which will be played twice. After you have clapped it, say if it is in two time, three time or four time.

Andante

Mozart

C1 *Questions*

    a. Does the **tempo** vary, or stay the same?

    b. Comment of the use of **dynamics**.

    c. Is the **tonality** major, or minor?

    d. What do you feel is the **character** of the piece?

    e. In what **style** and **period** do you think it was written?

C2 Clap this extract, which will be played twice. After you have clapped it, say if it is in two time, three time or four time.

C1 Questions

    a. Is the **texture** of this mostly homophonic, or contrapuntal?

    b. Is there any relationship between the **melody** of treble and bass in the first bars?

    c. Does the **tempo** remain the same, or does it vary?

    d. Is there any variation in the **dynamics**?

    e. In what **period** might it have been written?

C2 Clap this extract, which will be played twice. After you have clapped it, say if it is in two time, three time or four time.

Prokofiev (1881-1953)

C1 *Questions*

    a. Is the **articulation** at the beginning *staccato* or *legato*? Is it the same throughout?

    b. Describe the **dynamics** of the piece.

    c. Does the **tempo** alter, or stay the same?

    d. Comment on the **form** of the music.

    e. What is its musical **style** and **period**?

C2 Clap this extract, which will be played twice. After you have clapped it, say if it is in two time, three time or four time.

Andante

Hoffstetter (1742-1815)

12

simile

(This piece is sometimes attributed to Haydn)

C1 *Questions*
   a. Is this in major or minor **tonality**?
   b. Does the **tempo** alter or remain steady?
   c. Is the **articulation** of the upper part the same as the lower? If not, what happens?
   d. What is its musical **style** and **period**?

C2 Clap this extract, which will be played twice. After you have clapped it, say if it is in two time, three time or four time.

Grave

D. Scarlatti (1685-1757)

13 f (repeat p)

2nda volta rit.

C1 *Questions*

    a. Is this in major or minor **tonality**?

    b. Does the **tempo** alter or remain steady?

    c. Do the **dynamics** stay the same throughout? If not, what happens?

    d. What is its musical **style** and **period**?

C2 Clap this extract, which will be played twice. After you have clapped it, say if it is in two time, three time or four time.

C1 *Questions*

    a. Does this start in major or minor **tonality**?

    b. Describe the **dynamics** of the piece.

    c. Does the **tempo** alter, or stay the same?

    d. Comment on the **form** of the music. Is any part of it repeated?

    e. What is its musical **style** and **period**?

    f. Which word best describes the piece – (i) Waltz; (ii) March; (iii) Minuet?

C2 Clap this extract, which will be played twice. After you have clapped it, say if it is in two time, three time or four time.

Animato ♩. = 63

Schumann

C1 *Questions*

    a. Does this start in major or minor **tonality**?

    b. Describe the **dynamics** of the piece.

    c. Does the **tempo** alter, or stay the same?

    d. Comment on the **form** of the music. Is any part of it repeated?

    e. What is its musical **style** and **period**?

C2 Clap this extract, which will be played twice. After you have clapped it, say if it is in two time, three time or four time.

Con moto ♩ = 108-116

Claude Daquin (1694-1772)

16

p leggiero

C1 *Questions*
- a. Is the **tonality** of this major or minor?
- b. **Texture**. Comment on the lower part.
- c. Does the **tempo** alter, or stay the same?
- d. How often do you hear the **melody** of the first four-bar phrase?
- e. What is its musical **style** and **period** ?

C2 Clap this extract, which will be played twice. After you have clapped it, say if it is in two time, three time or four time.

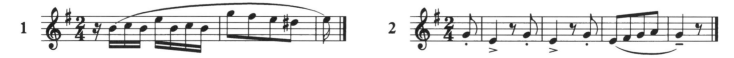

1

2

C1 *Questions*
   a. Does this end in major or minor **tonality**?
   b. Comment on the **rhythm** of the piece.
   c. Is the **harmony** simple, or rather unusual?
   d. Describe the **form** of the piece.
   e. What is its musical **style** and **period**?

C2 Clap this extract, which will be played twice. After you have clapped it, say if it is in two time, three time or four time.

C1 *Questions*

    a. Is the **tonality** at the end of this major or minor?

    b. Is the **texture** homophonic or contrapuntal?

    c. Does the **tempo** alter, or stay the same? What word would describe the tempo chosen?

    d. Is the **articulation** of the notes *staccato* or *legato*?

    e. What is its musical **style** and **period**?

C2 Clap this extract, which will be played twice. After you have clapped it, say if it is in two time, three time or four time.

C1 *Questions*
   a. Does this start in major or minor **tonality**?
   b. Comment on the **dynamics** of the piece.
   c. Does the **tempo** alter, or stay the same?
   d. Is the **texture** homophonic or contrapuntal?
   e. What is its musical **style** and **period**?

C2 Clap this extract, which will be played twice. After you have clapped it, say if it is in two time, three time or four time.

Appendix. Comments on the styles and periods of pieces in Section C.

No. 1 Uncomplicated harmony. Melodic phrases well balanced. Some contrasts in dynamics, but no violent ones. Classical in style and period.

No. 2 Texture often contrapuntal, with some imitation. Steady tempo. Terraced dynamics. Late Renaissance/early Baroque.

No. 3 Texture homophonic. Harmony uncomplicated. Wide variations in dynamics, and very expressive in mood. Romantic music.

No. 4 Steady tempo, and terraced dynamics. Some contrapuntal writing. Baroque style and period.

No. 5 Tempo steady. Dynamics varied, but not excessively. Harmony uncomplicated, and a general sense of restraint. Classical/early Romantic in style and period.

No. 6 Very fluid tempo. Harmony and key unusual. Modern in style and period.

No. 7 Steady in tempo. Harmony uncomplicated. Balanced in form. Classical in style and period.

No. 8 Very varied in dynamics and tempo. Harmony uncomplicated. Contemplative in mood, and Romantic in style and period.

No. 9 Varied dynamics, but the changes not dramatic. Tempo steady, and harmony uncomplicated. Phrases very well balanced. Classical in style and period.

No. 10 No tempo changes. Terraced dynamics. Imitative, contrapuntal writing. Baroque style and period.

No. 11 Unusual in harmony and a number of chromatic notes. Wide range of tone colour, and in the range of the notes used. Modern in style and period.

No. 12 Uncomplicated harmony. Steady tempo. Well-balanced phrases. No imitation or counterpoint. Classical in style and period.

No. 13 Steady tempo. Terraced dynamics. Baroque in style and period.

No. 14 Well-balanced phrases. Dynamics varied, but not excessively. Uncomplicated harmony. Classical in style and period.

No. 15 Wide contrasts in dynamics, and some fairly thick chords. Much use of pedal. Romantic in style and period.

No. 16 Very steady tempo apart from *rit.* at the end. No big contrasts in dynamics. Ornaments. Baroque/early Classical.

No. 17 Unusual chords and a great deal of syncopation. Modern in style and period.

No. 18 Steady in tempo, and dynamics unvaried. Some imitation and contrapuntal writing. Ornaments on left hand notes. Baroque in style and period.

No. 19 Very varied in dynamics and texture. Some thick, rich-sounding chords. Harmony fairly uncomplicated. Romantic in style and period.

Other titles by David Turnbull...

Theory Time!
Grade 5
BOE004908

Scale Time!
Grade 5
BOE005001

Available from

BOSWORTH
part of The Music Sales Group

Exclusive Distributors:
Music Sales Limited
Distribution Centre, Newmarket Road,
Bury St Edmunds, Suffolk IP33 3YB, UK.

www.musicsales.com